EXPL
BEAU.. WITHIN

Includes Several Powerful Meditation Techniques to Help You Discover Your Profound Inner Nature

JOHN H MOELLER

ISBN: 9798357605962

Printed in the United States of America

TABLE OF CONTENTS

INTRODUCTION

There is spectacular Beauty inside each and every one of us. It becomes clearer when the mind is quiet. When all the mud settles to the bottom, it is finally revealed. This is the beauty of a pure, kind heart and a still, peaceful mind. We don't always notice this beauty because of all the noise in our lives. If we don't pause to be silent we may only notice it on rare occasions. When we go for a hike and pause to view a beautiful mountain scene, we feel peaceful, calm, inspired. This can be compared to what we view with our eyes closed while in meditation, yet in this context, it is even more profound and meaningful. We can pause and take in the inner beauty, which is our true nature. The great vistas within are always there but we only see them clearly when we quiet our minds.

These experiences into our inner nature are not only beautiful but very powerful and impactful. Over time, these experiences rewire the brain and can cause these inner qualities to be manifested in one's day-to-day life, making them permanent traits. I invite you to embark on this wonderful journey and explore the beauty within yourself.

In this small book, I share my experience of exploring various meditation techniques, most of which I have created myself. In doing so, I hope to inspire you to do something similar. The 39 meditation techniques in Chapter 5 and the additional routines in Chapter 6 are valuable practices with something for everyone. Whether you are new at meditation or have been practicing for years, these techniques are suitable for all skill levels.

ACKNOWLEDGEMENTS

I would like to thank my dear friends who attend the weekly guided meditations that I lead. I appreciate the many discussions we have had. Their insights and feedback have been extremely valuable.

CHAPTER 1
THE JOURNEY BEGINS

When I was living in Albuquerque, NM, back in 2013, I decided to do an experiment. Each month I would try a new religion. I would do whatever practices that particular religion did and attend their meetings. Since there were some Buddhist sanghas in town, I started there. I began to attend a sangha that I liked, once or twice a week, and I started a daily practice of meditation. When the month was up, I found that I was very happy with this discipline. So I decided to end my experiment right there and then and simply continue my newfound practice. Although I never actually became a Buddhist, I found the teachings were thought-provoking, and Buddhists were very accepting of me. Even though I have other beliefs, I've always felt that I was accepted just as much as a fellow Buddhist. The main thing that I liked about Buddhism was meditation. Even before I attended Buddhist meetings, I meditated off and on and realized that it was a very effective practice. Now it became a daily practice and has remained that way to this day.

As I attended various sanghas and read some books by Buddhist, Hindu, and other spiritual authors, I realized there are several ways to meditate. The Buddha himself taught many types of meditation. So I began experimenting with various techniques. From the knowledge I gained, I already had a handful of techniques to practice. I wanted to expand upon this. So I did a Google search and I discovered an excellent website called LiveAndDare.com, authored by Giovanni Dienstmann.

https://liveanddare.com/types-of-meditation/

The link above is a page on his website entitled, "Types of Meditation: An Overview of 23 Meditation Techniques." On this page, there are techniques from various religions: Buddhism, Hinduism, Taoism, Christianity, and Sufism. Here is a quote from that web page:

"There are literally hundreds—if not thousands—of types of meditation, so here I will explore only the most popular ones. The purpose of this article is to help you experiment with different meditation techniques, and find the ones that work best for you... You need to experiment with many, and find the one that works best for your unique needs and personality."[1]   -
Giovanni Dienstmann

This is exactly how I felt about meditation, so it really resonated with me. I selected some techniques from this page to try out. I also added some techniques that I already knew of from Buddhism, other traditions, and some of my own ideas. Some of these ideas were influenced by books I read as well as teachers that I learned from locally. Some ideas actually came to me as I meditated. I started with about 30 techniques to work with. My goal was to find a handful of techniques that worked well for me that I could practice regularly. I have found that the enjoyment of this exercise has actually caused me to change my goal for this experiment as well, much like my experiment with different religions. I spend more time now experimenting with new techniques than I do practicing my favorite ones. I really don't mind. I love seeing the effect they have on me and I feel that I benefit from constantly trying new meditations.

CHAPTER 2
SOME THOUGHTS ON MEDITATION

Your True Nature

Meditation helps reveal your true nature... or in Buddhist lingo, your Buddha nature. Kindness, love, peace, and well-being can come forth as we still our minds. With the clutter gone, our true nature can be realized. The following quotes are from the Hindu monk, Om Swami, a bestselling author of more than fifteen books on meditation, wellness, and spirituality.

> *"Meditation is about discovering your natural state of peace and bliss."*[2]
> -Om Swami (A Million Thoughts)

> *"A mind that has gone empty fills with love naturally."*[3]
> -Om Swami (A Million Thoughts)

An Enjoyable Experience

Meditation should be an enjoyable experience. That does not mean we won't have some difficulty getting there, but with practice, the more proficient we become at meditation the more pleasurable it becomes.

> *"Practice should be enjoyable and pleasant. It should be full of joy."*[4]
> -Thich Nhat Hahn (You Are Here)

Making it Interesting

Thich Nhat Hanh was a Vietnamese Thien Buddhist monk who recently passed away. He was, and still is, one of the most quoted teachers in modern-day Buddhism. He was a prolific author and founder of the Plum Village Tradition. In a speech given in France in 2005, he explains the importance of making meditation interesting. He compares meditation to an interesting speech. He mentions that even though you may not have slept well the night before, yet if you listen to an interesting speech, you find that you are alert. The opposite is also true: If you had a good night's sleep and then listen to a boring speech you will feel sleepy. It is the same with meditation. If you make your meditation interesting you will be more alert and more focused. He says, "I also in the past I have fought a lot to stay awake during sitting. But I have found out that struggling like that does not bring any results... You have to make your sitting interesting, into a blessing... To make the practice interesting, to make the practice enjoyable, that is the answer. That is the best way, the only way to fight against sleepiness."[5]

The monk, Ajahn Brahm, who is an author and the abbot at a Theravada Buddhist monastery in Western Australia, also spoke to the importance of making meditation interesting. In speaking about breathing meditation, he said, "Adding something extra to the breathing makes it more interesting and easy for you to observe."[6] He was speaking about the Anapanasati Sutta which, in steps 1 and 2, instructs the meditator to observe whether the breath is short or long. He says that this is just one way to make meditation more interesting. He also mentioned one way in which he teaches breathing meditation: When you inhale, breathe in peace, and when you exhale tell yourself to "let go."[6]

It is helpful to be creative in making your meditation interesting. Later in this booklet, as I present some techniques, you will see plenty of examples of this. You can make your meditations interesting by trying some of your own ideas for meditation. It has been my experience that the more different types of techniques you try, the more your own creativity will begin to kick in. Be curious and ask yourself, "What would happen if I tried this or that in my meditation practice?"

Spiritual Insights

I mentioned that many of the ideas for meditation techniques that I created came to me as I was meditating. This is one example of insights that might occur during meditation. In the Hindu scripture, the Bhagavad Gita, Krishna mentions that a heart that has found quietness allows wisdom to come forth.

> *"In this quietness falls down the burden of all her sorrows, for when the heart has found quietness, wisdom has also found peace."* [7]
> -Bhagavad Gita 2:65

You Can't Go Wrong!

There is no such thing as a bad meditation session. A successful meditation is one for which you showed up. Even during a difficult meditation, where the mind frequently wanders, every time we bring the mind back to the object of our meditation, we are training our minds. The object of meditation might be the breath, the body, a mantra, or various other things that one might use as the focus of meditation.

This training of the mind can be compared to exercising the body. When we exercise the body we might, at times, have a difficult workout. We might not even feel like working out, but because we make the effort to show up at the gym, the result will be stronger muscles over time. In the same way, when we meditate we are exercising the mind, and over time, the mind becomes stronger and healthier.

A Well-Rounded Work-Out

Working with multiple techniques can affect different aspects of your mind and heart. Let's continue with the analogy of exercising. A bodybuilder doesn't only do one type of exercise. No, he will build up arm muscles like the triceps with tricep curls. He will also do military presses to work out his shoulders. In fact, he will do a different exercise for each muscle in the body. In the same way, some meditation techniques specifically focus on developing love and kindness. Others may focus mainly on quieting the mind. Some may help develop other qualities, like joy, gratitude, peace, etc.

Rewiring the Mind

 *"When neuroscientists tested expert meditators, they discovered something surprising: The effect of Buddhist meditation isn't just momentary; it can alter deep-seated traits in our brain patterns and character."[8]*

https://www.lionsroar.com/how-meditation-changes-your-brain-and-your-life/

This quote is from the introduction to an article from the Lion's Roar website. The article "How Meditation Changes Your Brain — and Your Life," written by neuroscientists Daniel Goleman and Richard Davidson, introduces the research they have done and the book they have written concerning this research. This book is entitled "Altered Traits: Science Reveals How Meditation Changes Your Mind, Brain, and Body."[9]

Consistency Pays Off

Just as with anything, the more consistent you are with your practice the greater the results. Someone challenged me a long time ago to spend at least five minutes a day in some kind of spiritual practice. I didn't realize at the time what sort of effect that would have on me. I thought that would be easy, just five minutes!

So that's what I did. However, those five minutes every day caused me to hunger for more until it became an hour each day. I may spend 30 minutes in the morning practicing sitting meditation. Then in the afternoon I might go for a walk outside and fill it with meditation and prayer. So if you don't already have a daily practice of meditation and feel overwhelmed by doing it every day, then try the five-minute approach and see if you also begin to hunger for more.

> *"Day after day, let the Yogi practice the harmony of soul: in a secret place, in deep solitude, master of his mind, hoping for nothing, desiring nothing."*[10]   -Bhagavad Gita 6:10

CHAPTER 3
BASIC TRAINING

Before we get into my experiment with meditation and my top 39 techniques, I would like to provide you with some basics of meditation. If you are a new meditator it might be a good idea to start here before getting into the techniques that will be presented in Chapter 5. Once you get the hang of it, then you can move on to the rest of the book.

The goals of meditation are to quiet the mind, reduce stress, gain insight, cultivate positive qualities such as love, kindness, joy, and peace, and ultimately attain enlightenment. As a result, a person who meditates will over time become more peaceful, happy, and wise.

To begin any meditation session it is important to find a place that is quiet and free from distractions. If this is not entirely possible then please work with what you have. Whatever distractions are there that you cannot change, please try to accept them and be at peace with your situation.

You can either sit on a chair or cross-legged on the ground. It is important to maintain good posture. Make sure that you are sitting up straight, but not too rigid. Your body should be relaxed. You may need to remind yourself of your posture from time to time throughout your meditation and make adjustments as needed. A good posture helps you to stay alert. Often at the beginning of my meditation sessions, I will focus on my posture for about a minute, just being mindful of it, and observing it as the object of my meditation. This helps to establish the posture for the remainder of the time.

I recommend that you close your eyes during meditation. However, if you would like to experiment and try with your eyes open there is no harm in this, so long as it does not become a distraction. Sometimes it can be helpful to open your eyes for a short while if you feel sleepy to help you stay alert.

When it comes to sleepiness, there are different ways to deal with this. I have included some meditations in Chapter 5 called "High Energy" meditations, which will raise your energy level. You can use the techniques as tools in your arsenal to deal with drowsiness. If sleepiness is too overwhelming, it is okay to stand up for a while while you meditate to help get your blood flowing.

 Most meditation techniques have a few things in common. Most have an anchor. An anchor is a point of focus. One of the most common anchors for many meditators is the breath. When you use the breath as an anchor you observe the breath without controlling

it in any way. This focus helps to quiet the mind. If the mind gets lost in thought or begins to wander you simply bring your attention back to the breath. It is important not to get upset or impatient when the mind wanders. The idea is to be gentle with the mind. It's common, especially for beginners, for the mind to wander several times during the meditation session. Keep in mind, though, that every time you let go of the thoughts and come back to the anchor you are training the mind.

Another common anchor for many meditators is a word or a phrase called a mantra. Most people are familiar with the mantra, "*Om*." The word "*Om*" is repeated silently or out loud and you focus on the word as it is repeated. It is the same as focusing on the breath. Whenever the mind wanders you bring your attention back to the mantra. There are probably thousands of mantras that can be used. You could even use a mantra with a meaning such as the words "calm" or "kindness."

The body is another common anchor. You focus on the body and bodily sensations.

Another anchor commonly used is the mind itself. You simply observe the mind. If the mind is busy with thoughts you just watch the thoughts but don't get caught up in them. If the mind is quiet then you observe the silence. If the mind is peaceful, or if it is agitated, you observe that as well.

Another anchor may be just whatever comes to your awareness during your session. So as you meditate you might notice thoughts, sensations, emotions, or even qualities such as peace or stress. The anchor may change throughout the session. This is perfectly okay. Whatever comes to your awareness in the moment is the anchor and that's likely to change.

CHAPTER 4
MEDITATION LABORATORY

Now that you have an understanding of some of the basics of meditation, I will continue to explain my ongoing experiment. For myself, when I sit down to meditate, I am not only enjoying a peaceful and beneficial meditation session but I am also entering into my meditation laboratory. Just as some medical laboratories try to discover cures for diseases, I discover effective meditation techniques to help to cure mental and emotional suffering while bringing inner peace and happiness. As I said earlier, my experiment is to test and evaluate many different types of meditation, not just traditional techniques, but also techniques that I create myself.

As a disclaimer, there is a part of me that is rather analytical and methodical. So this section may not appeal to everyone. Some people may not like the idea of ranking their meditation and that's fine. This is more of a "For What it's Worth" section. It may be something you will want to try if you are geared that way, or you can discount it altogether if you like. If you like the idea of experimenting with various styles of meditation then this is one way to evaluate them.

One advantage I have found that helps me is that by using this ranking system, I am giving myself a measurable assignment, which causes me to become more focused during meditation, especially when I track the results afterward on a spreadsheet. So there is something of an accountability factor in this way.

If you should decide to create your own meditation technique this system of evaluation could be helpful. Some ideas may seem good at first, but then it seems the more you try them the less effective they are. They produce diminishing returns. Many ideas have a placebo effect. They work at first, but if there is not enough substance to them then they eventually drop out. A really good meditation technique should work consistently over time, not just for a while. Sometimes even if it is a good meditation technique it might not be a good fit for you personally, and this evaluation system will weed out these bad fits as well.

To evaluate the meditations, I do a 20-minute session with each technique and rate them from 0 to 10; 10 being the best. I use the following chart as a guide:

10 = Excellent

9

8 = Very good

7

6 = Good

5

4 = Okay

3

2 = So-so

1

0 = No way!

The question might be asked, "Why not just rank 0-5 since half of these values don't have adjectives?" One reason is because it is helpful when you can't decide which rank to give something. For example, you might be torn between giving a particular meditation either a 6 (good) or an 8 (very good,) which happens frequently. In this case you could give it a 7. A 7 therefore would be half way between good and very good. Plus it helps to have a wider range of values when figuring out averages.

Each meditation has to achieve a certain score during each round or be eliminated. For example, after two sessions with a technique, the average score per round must be at least 4, which is just "okay." Then I make it a little harder with each round. In this manner, I am lenient during the first 5 tries with each technique. If they are not eliminated after 5 tries, then I make the requirement tougher. So on the sixth try and thereafter they have to maintain an average score of at least 7, which according to my chart is between "good" and "very good."

Ajahn Brahm uses what he calls a "peace-o-meter." He often rates his meditations from 1 to 10 in much the same way as I do. He asks the question, "What attitude of mind is needed to move that needle (of the peace-o-meter) closer and closer to peace?" [11]

Meditations Still Standing

After having done this for 9 years, I have evaluated nearly 400 techniques. There are only 39 that have not been eliminated, even after trying them many times. This is not to say that these techniques will be just as effective for everyone else who tries them. The only way to know if they work for you is to try them out yourself. The following chapter explains these techniques, and I encourage you to try and see if any of these are a good fit for you.

CHAPTER 5
THE TOP 39 MEDITATION TECHNIQUES

They say that variety is the spice of life, and I believe this applies to meditation as well. If you have several meditation techniques to work with, it can be very effective to do a different one each day and then start over when you have done them all. This keeps your practice interesting and exciting.

There are a couple of words that I use in this chapter that can be misunderstood since they tend to have more than one meaning. Below I explain my intention in using them:

Beauty:
In this chapter, "beauty" and "beautiful" are used in the sense that peace, bliss, and silence are beautiful. When the mind is still and peaceful we become aware of sensations or feelings, and they seem very beautiful in this heightened state of awareness. This is the power of mindfulness. It changes the mundane into something beautiful. In meditation, we may also experience feelings of love and kindness that also seem so beautiful. If I say "beautiful body" I am not referring to the attractiveness of the body or anything related to the ego. What I mean is the body is a beautiful focus of meditation.

Power:

In using the word "power" or "powerful," it is not in the worldly sense in which the ego is fed. We often refer to people as being very powerful. This might mean they have a lot of money and influence. If we say this person has a very powerful body it means they are very strong. These connotations are not intended for usage in this chapter. Rather, power is referring to the kind of effect that a particular focus of meditation is having on you. An example would be "a powerful silence." This would mean the silence has a powerful effect on you. In the meditation called "Sacred Adjectives for the Body;" for example, the phrase "powerful body" is used. I don't mean it is strong, rather that using the body as a focus of meditation has a powerful effect.

Sacred:

For some people a certain day of the week or a certain holiday is sacred. Many people make pilgrimages to a certain place because they believe it is sacred ground. A saintly person may be considered sacred or holy by some. In each of these cases, the object that is considered sacred is held in very high esteem in a deeply spiritual sense. In the same way, we can see our time in meditation as being very sacred or holy. Whenever we take time to still our minds we are creating a sacred moment. When we focus on an anchor like the breath, the mind, the body or the moment, the attention we give it makes the anchor sacred. Spiritual qualities that we observe during meditation can be considered sacred, such as silence, peace, kindness, or joy. It is truly a powerful practice to see our time in meditation as being sacred, holy, or divine.

When you try the following techniques I recommend that you meditate for about 20 minutes. The first three minutes should be a warm-up. So before you start the actual technique, just settle in by focusing on your breath, body, or mind. Once you feel at least somewhat settled you can begin the technique.

So here are my favorite techniques. I hope they are as much a blessing to you as they have been for me.

The Power of Positive Adjectives

Certain words can have a powerful effect on the mind. The following techniques demonstrate how powerful the right adjectives can be to bring us to a deeper state of consciousness.

Positive Feedback

After the three-minute warm-up, you should begin to settle into your meditation. If you notice peace, stillness, or any pleasant sensation, say to yourself, "good," "excellent," or any positive word of encouragement. Continue to do this throughout your time meditating. I've found that it helps to not use the same feedback word all the time. Try to mix it up a bit with words such as good, very good, excellent, yes, nice, etc.

I have found that this meditation causes me to experience more peace, more pleasant sensations, more quietness of mind, and deeper meditation. It's as if my subconscious mind takes encouragement from this positive feedback.

Sacred Adjectives

I have found this to be a very powerful technique. Be sure to begin with a few minutes of warm-up as I described in the intro to this section. As you settle into your meditation, you should begin to feel calmer, quieter, and more peaceful. At this point, begin this technique by using adjectives that positively describe your experience. Below is a list of adjectives that you might want to try. Simply run these adjectives through your mind. You can even try them if you don't necessarily feel that way, just to see what effect it has on you. Mindfully take your time with each word. Savor each adjective as if each one is very sacred, and truly they are. All these qualities describe what is already there within us. However, we are normally distracted from the truth of who we really are. This technique helps us wake up to our true nature, so when you use adjectives such as "powerful," "sacred," or "beautiful," you are not exaggerating.

Quiet	Healing	Sacred	Pure
Heavenly	Blissful	Powerful	Precious
Gentle	Still	Happy	Loving
Perfect	Peaceful	Divine	Beautiful
Kind	Tender	Calm	Joyful

Many of the meditation descriptions in this chapter contain lists similar to this. Whenever there is a list please feel free to include your own adjectives or in some cases nouns. Also, if any of the words I have listed do not resonate with you after a few attempts then feel free to exclude them.

Sacred Adjectives for Specific Focuses (9 applications)

Now that you understand how the Sacred Adjective meditation works, you can also apply the adjectives to specific focuses (anchors.) The focuses that have worked the best for me are **the body, the mind, the moment, awareness, sensations, silence, bliss, kindness, and yourself.** So here you have nine different meditations that you can try.

You can say, "This **body** is a calm body, this body is a peaceful place, this body is beautiful," etc. In other words just fill in the blank with a positive, meaningful adjective, "This body is _____." For "Sacred Adjectives for **Yourself**" you would say, "I am precious, I am blissful, etc." Of course do **awareness**, **quietness**, and the others in the same fashion, just applying the adjectives to them as you see fit.

What I mean by "a **sensation**" is whatever sensation that you may feel in the moment. You might feel a pleasant, peaceful sensation in your body which often arises as your mind becomes quiet. You might feel a certain energy in your body or a tingling sensation. Whatever the case may be, just apply the adjectives. Even try some of these adjectives if you don't feel that way and see what effect it has. Some examples would be, "This sensation is a calm sensation, a peaceful sensation, a blissful sensation," etc.

There are so many ways to apply this method. I would encourage you to try to apply sacred adjectives to other focuses that I have not mentioned and come up with your own creation.

I did a guided meditation once on "Sacred Adjectives for the Mind," for the Buddhist sangha that I attend. One

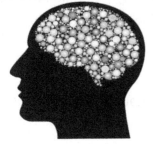

friend told me sometime later that, at first, she could not relate to this technique. I would say phrases like, "This mind is a quiet place ...a peaceful place ...a beautiful mind." She told me that she

30

could not relate to these phrases because her mind didn't feel that way. She felt that the mind was more of an obstacle to meditation. In this sense, it was not at all quiet, peaceful or beautiful. Once she caught on though, this technique became very powerful for her. By interjecting these suggestions she began to see that the mind can indeed be beautiful and an aid to meditation rather than a hindrance. Certainly, the mind can be very busy and it can be hard for it to settle, but once it does settle it can be a very peaceful place, even blissful.

On another occasion, I did a guided meditation for "Sacred Adjectives for Sensations." I normally focus on pleasant sensations in the body. As I led the small group, I asked them to focus on a pleasant sensation in the body, then I repeated phrases for them to work with such as, "This sensation is a calm sensation, a beautiful sensation, a peaceful sensation." After the meditation session, we discussed our experience working with this technique. One friend in the group, Monty, had been dealing with ongoing pain in his body and he found it difficult to even find a pleasant sensation. So he applied the adjectives to the sensation of pain he was feeling. He found it to be very effective in dealing with his pain. He especially found the phrase, "This sensation is a sacred sensation," helpful. This is what he said, "I had this sense that pain is sacred because it's also a part of the flow of existence... So, thinking of pain as sacred is a reminder that it, too, is a manifestation of divinity. During our meditation, this helped me to lean into and accept the pain as part of my practice, rather than taking my habitual route of attempting to avoid it."

Sacred Adjectives for Various Anchors

As you might recall in Chapter 3, an anchor is something you focus on during your meditation. Examples are the breath, the body, the mind, the moment, etc. So with this meditation, you will use sacred adjectives with several anchors. So you might start with the body, and then transition at some point to the mind, then the moment, and so on. You could transition systematically like this or you can transition as you feel moved. What I mean is, if you are applying adjectives to the body, and then feel that your mind is very peaceful, you could start saying, "This mind is a beautiful mind, a sacred mind," etc. You could also try using one adjective for a while and applying it to each focus: "This body is a peaceful place, this mind is a peaceful place, this moment is a peaceful moment, I am peaceful," and so on.

Sacred Adjectives for Spiritual Qualities

In this meditation, we use spiritual qualities as anchors and apply sacred adjectives to them. Some examples of this are "Beautiful silence," "sacred peace," "powerful kindness," "divine love," etc. Below is a list of spiritual qualities to which you can apply sacred adjectives.

Kindness	Silence	Pureness	Happiness
Gentleness	Peace	Joy	Stillness
Bliss	Tenderness	Love	

Precious

This technique will help you see all things in your awareness as being very precious. Use the word "precious" to describe your experience as you meditate. Practice seeing everything that you notice as being very precious; things such as your body, breath, mind, the moment, your heart, sensations, emotions, and even your awareness. In fact, everything that you notice during your session can be seen as being very precious. Below are some things the word "precious" can be applied to.

Calm	Silence	Awareness	Mind
Beauty	Moment	Peace	Sacredness
Power	Stillness	Bliss	Love
Joy	Breath	Kindness	Body
Heart	Sensations		

Beautiful!

This meditation helps you to see the beauty within. You simply use phrases that emphasize the beauty of inner spiritual qualities or meditation anchors such as the breath, the mind, the body, and the moment. To create these phrases you fill in the blank for this phrase: "This is a beautiful _____!" You can use the same list given in the "Precious" meditation technique.

Incredible!

In this technique use the word "incredible" to describe various things that you may become aware of during your meditation. Examples: Incredible peace, incredible silence, incredible love, incredible body, incredible mind, incredible beauty, etc. Again, I feel it's very important to remind you that this should not be seen as an exaggeration. All these qualities and focuses are, in reality, quite incredible! So this meditation should help you to see them as such, rather than falling into the trap of taking them for granted, as we all tend to do. You can use the same list under the Precious meditation to which you can apply this adjective.

Super Charged Adjectives for Spiritual Qualities

Just like the word "incredible," there are other adjectives that take it up a notch while not being an exaggeration but instead a reality when it comes to the spiritual qualities that are within you. Here we use strong adjectives such as profound, amazing, spectacular, etc to describe our spiritual superpowers such as love, kindness, peace, silence, etc. This helps us to wake up to the fact that they are indeed amazing and phenomenal qualities. Below are some supercharged adjectives that can be used.

Incredible	Powerful	Profound
Supernatural	Exquisite	Limitless
Immeasurable	Deep	Unbelievable
Spectacular	Phenomenal	Miraculous

These adjectives can be applied to any of the qualities in the list under the "Precious" meditation. Some examples are "powerful silence," "unbelievable kindness," "profound beauty," "spectacular bliss," etc.

Quotations

A very effective technique is to use a favorite quote from an inspirational source. It could be from scripture that you hold dear, or from any inspirational book. Below are some quotes that I have found very effective. They are from the Hindu scripture, the Bhagavad Gita, translated by Juan Mascaro. In these meditations, you should first memorize the verse. Once you have the words mastered simply repeat them mindfully and allow them to sink in. You can also notice how it feels in your body to hear them.

Harmony of Mind

Verse 17:16

> "Quietness of mind, silence, self-harmony, loving-kindness, and a pure heart. This is the harmony of the mind."[12]

The Sage of Silence

Verse 5:27-28

> "When the sage of silence... closes the doors of his soul... keeps peaceful and even the ebbing and flowing of breath... keeps silent his soul."[13]

Adoration and Harmony

Verse 9:22

> "To those who adore me with a pure oneness of soul, to those who are ever in harmony, I increase what they have and I give them what they have not."[14]

Some of you might ask, "Does meditation deal at all with belief in God?" Certainly, meditation is a deeply spiritual practice. Buddhist meditation never mentions anything about God, whereas some Hindu meditations do indeed focus on God. I personally believe in God, but I have a deep respect for Buddhist practitioners, many of whom are deeply spiritual. Could it be that what they are experiencing is all about God, yet they don't necessarily call it as such or view it that way? Or perhaps could it also be that those who believe in God are actually just in touch with some sort of unexplainable reality that is easily explained as a personal, all-knowing, and all-powerful Being? Well, I don't know the answers to these questions, but this is one possible explanation. With this in mind, I would like to comment briefly on this quotation.

This verse from the Bhagavad Gita is spoken by Krishna. A Hindu may read this and have no trouble with it. Hindus believe in one God who reveals himself in many ways. In other words, when a Hindu worships Krishna he is actually worshiping the one God over all who is manifesting Himself as Krishna. With this in mind, I would like to offer three different approaches to meditation on this verse:

1. The Hindu approach: Adore Krishna, knowing that it is the same as adoring God.
2. Adoring God according to your concept of God or a higher power
3. Look at the speaker of this verse as a *personification* of whatever you see the ultimate reality of life to be. So with this approach, there is no worship of a higher being involved. You are not using "*adore*" in the sense of worship.

I truly believe that this verse is powerful no matter which approach you use. I debated whether or not to include this verse in this book, because, as you see, it requires some explanation. Yet, I believe this verse is very much worth the extra commentary. I hope you see it that way as well when you use it as a focus of your meditation.

I would also like to comment on the last phrase of the verse. *"I increase what they have and I give them what they have not."* I think the things that will *increase* are mainly spiritual growth, and "what they have not" may refer to enlightenment. That's not to say that you might also experience an increase in achievements and physical things. After all, if you are "*ever in harmony*" it is likely that you will benefit in many ways since you will be a very stable person. A stable mind is very focused which can make you very capable of accomplishing much. However, any physical gains should be looked at as a fringe benefit and not the main goal of this verse.

Feeling Good!

The following techniques are about finding pleasant feelings or sensations that are present within you. You will probably notice that some of the "Feeling Good" meditations are very similar. I admit they are, but I find that the choice of words you use to help you focus on the pleasant feelings can make a big difference in your meditation experience. So one phrase such as "Follow your bliss" might have a different effect than focusing on the phrase "Feelings of bliss" even though the idea is similar.

Mindfulness of Any Peace That Arises

Be mindful whenever you feel even the slightest peace while you are meditating. Let that be the focus of your meditation. Be focused on the peace you feel as you would your breath in a breathing meditation. Stay with that peace. Follow it. What does it feel like? Be curious.

The Body Filled With Bliss

This technique is from a Hindu scripture called "Vijnanabhairava Tantra." This is one of several meditation techniques from this source. In this meditation, one is instructed to feel or imagine that the body is filled with bliss.

"Contemplate on… one's own body as being filled with bliss."[15]

You may not feel any bliss or any pleasant sensation at first but start by using your imagination. Little by little it should feel more real. At least that has been my experience. If the word "bliss" seems too difficult for you to imagine, then start by just picturing that your body feels "good." You can then gradually work up to "bliss."

Feelings of Bliss

Be mindful of any blissful feeling you may have whether it be in the body or the mind or a general overall feeling. If you do not feel any bliss then try to imagine what bliss feels like. The imagination is often a good starting point. The more you can relax, the more readily blissful or pleasant feelings should arise.

Follow Your Bliss

I borrowed this phrase from the famous author, Joseph Campbell. Campbell uses this phrase to encourage us to make decisions in our lives that we are truly passionate about rather than keeping in line with the status quo.[16] However, my usage of it is different from Campbell's. It is in the context of meditation. So with this technique, you seek to find and follow your inner bliss in the moment. This normally starts with quieting your mind so it is important to do the warm-up for about three minutes so you can begin to feel calmer and quieter. Once you feel even the slightest sense of bliss, focus on it and follow it.

Explore Good Feelings that are Present

Be mindful of any good feelings or sensations that you notice, even if it's very slight. Just be with the feelings that are present, rather than trying to manufacture them.

<u>Body Work</u>

Pressure Points

Imagine that you are physically applying just the right amount of pressure to various points of your body with your imaginary hand as you meditate. Think of how a massage therapist might do this. Picture this gentle pressure releasing tension in your body. You can even imagine that you are sending positive energy into your body from that point. Allow this soothing pressure to relax, quiet, and calm you. If your mind begins to drift in thought, bring it back to the pressure points.

Spirit Hand

This one requires some imagination. Imagine that you are putting an invisible hand or hands into your body and with it you are sending your body positive spiritual energy. You can imagine this as your hand or God's hand, depending on your beliefs. Experiment with this by imagining this spirit hand going into your heart, head, spine, or anywhere else in your body.

High Energy

The following techniques are quite different from most traditional meditation techniques in that they are stimulating rather than calming.

These are good meditations, especially during times when you are sleepy. Om Swami says "If I were to sum up the art of meditation in one sentence, it would be, 'Exert when relaxed and relax when exerted.'"[17] These techniques are excellent for exerting when you are feeling drowsy and need to get your blood going. This is not to say that you cannot practice them when you are alert as well.

It's interesting what I find with all three of these exerting meditations. About halfway through the session, I often feel a deep sense of calm even while I am excited.

Infusion

Imagine that you are infusing positive spiritual energy into your body. You might start from the bottom of your belly and imagine the energy moving up your body, all the way to your head.

It's helpful to use your hands to help you focus. Start by having your hands open, palms up, and level with your belly button. Then move your hands up at a slow steady pace, just in front of the body, all the way to the head. Do this as if you are moving the energy with your hands into every cell in your body. You can do this several times, as needed to help you focus.

Excitement

Just feel excited! Feel the sensation of excitement. Don't think about anything specific that makes you excited unless it's excitement about this moment or life in general. I mention this because if you are thinking about excitement about various specific things then the mind tends to go off into thought about these things, but here the purpose is for the mind to remain excited, but not scattered. Let just the feeling of wholesome excitement be the focus of your meditation.

Rejoicing

In this meditation, you will simply be rejoicing. Just feel the sensation of rejoicing. I recommend that you even raise your arms above your head, off and on, throughout your meditation to express rejoicing. Let rejoicing be the focus of your meditation. Like the "Excitement" meditation, don't rejoice about anything specific. Just rejoice for the sake of rejoicing! I would also suggest that if you would like to experiment and try a "rejoicing" or an "excitement" meditation about various *specific* things, then I would encourage you to do so. See which one you enjoy more, and notice how they are different.

Other Techniques

Stuff Happens

I first heard of a technique that emphasized that "Breathing is *happening*." I expanded this concept a bit here to include other things in one's awareness that are also happening.

In this meditation, the focus is on the fact that things are happening in our awareness and that we are just observing them happen. It can make a big difference to think "breathing is happening" rather than thinking "I am breathing." In this example, we are focusing more on the breathing taking place rather than "I am the one breathing."

Below is a list of things to observe that "are happening." With these words, you can simply fill in the blank for the phrase "_____ is/are happening." Of course, please use your own words as well if you like. You can use anything that comes to your awareness. So if you become aware that you are feeling a positive quality such as kindness, you can say "kindness is happening."

Breathing	Sitting	Sensations
Awareness	Thoughts	Silence
Calm	This Moment	Peace
Sounds	Emotions	Difficulty

Metta

Metta is a Pali (ancient language at the time of the Buddha) word which means positive energy and kindness toward others. This is a very popular meditation that is from the Buddhist tradition. I have expanded upon it in a few small ways and I have also simplified it in other ways. Begin by taking a moment to wish yourself well. You can say, "May I be well. May I be happy." Then, for the rest of your meditation, wish others well. You might say may he/she be happy, healthy, wise, etc. You can also imagine that you are sending them positive spiritual energy. You can even imagine that you are placing your hand on someone's shoulder and sending transforming energy into their body. You can even include Christian-like prayer if you are so inclined. Do this for whoever you care about, family, friends, co-workers, etc. You might want to even try to send metta to people you might not care for so much, a difficult person. Doing the latter may be difficult at first, but it helps you to cultivate a love for all beings, not just those you are fond of.

Treasure Hunt

Within us are great treasures: precious gems of peace, quietness, beauty, kindness, love, stillness, etc. In this meditation, as the mind begins to be quiet and peaceful, we imagine that quietness and peace are precious gems. You can imagine putting these gems in a special pouch and becoming richer with each find. As you continue you may sense the beauty of the moment. This beauty is another precious gem that you gratefully collect. You may even sense the feelings of kindness or love and collect these special gems as well. You realize that with each gem you obtain, your wealth is growing. Continue in this way to find more rare and valuable gems. Continue to come across more peace, more silence, and more beauty. You may find other gems such as gentleness, tenderness, sacredness, joy, bliss, etc.

If you get stuck it's helpful to bring yourself back to silence. Many of these gems emerge when the mind is silent. Of course, silence is in itself a very precious gem. You could also work with an anchor such as the breath or the body to help to quiet the mind.

Harmony

Here we focus on being in harmony. You can use the word in general, sensing what it is like to be in harmony. You can also apply the word to various focuses so that you contemplate the mind being in harmony, the body, the breath, etc.

Breathe in Sacred Qualities

I'm not sure where this meditation originated but I have heard a few instructors teach it. Imagine you are breathing in wholesome qualities such as love, peace, kindness, etc. Imagine they are going to every part of your body, even every cell of the body. Here is a list of wholesome qualities that you might want to try.

Silence	Pureness	Happiness
Peace	Joy	Stillness
Bliss	Love	Tenderness
Kindness	Gentleness	Sacredness
Calm	Power	Beauty

Practice

Whenever we meditate, we are doing a practice, a practice with great benefits. This technique emphasizes the fact that we are practicing. There is no "good" or "bad" in practice. We are simply practicing to become more aware and to reap the benefits of mindfulness. When we practice anything we become better at it. In this technique, we fill in the blank of the short phrase "Practice _____." An example would be "practice peace," or "practice love." When we practice either of these qualities, we are sensing what it feels like to have peace within or feel love within. The following are words that you can use to fill in the blank. You don't have to use them all but pick a few that resonate with you or come up with some words of your own.

Observing	Awareness	Enjoying
Love	Breathing	Silence
Stillness	Smiling	Peace
Happiness	Joy	Kindness
Bliss	Feeling Good	

Sacred Qualities

With this technique, you are bringing to mind the various beautiful qualities of your true nature. Be sure to start your session with a few minutes of warm-up, as I have described at the beginning of this chapter. This allows for your sacred qualities to begin emerging. Then I recommend starting with the sacred quality of *silence* since a quiet mind is usually from where the other qualities are realized. *Calm* or *stillness* are also good starting points. Take a few seconds or a minute to focus on your inner quality of silence. Notice the feeling of silence in your mind and body. Then move on to other qualities such as *kindness, peace, love, and sacredness.* Below I have listed some other qualities that you can use. After you go through a few of the qualities it's okay to revisit some of them that resonated with you. It might be a good idea to read through the list of qualities before you start to meditate, rather than reading them as you meditate. But if your memory is not that good you could set the list next to you and occasionally take a peak.

Silence	Pureness	Happiness
Peace	Joy	Stillness
Bliss	Love	Tenderness
Kindness	Gentleness	Sacredness
Calm	Power	Beauty

One way to go about experiencing these sacred qualities is to go through them systematically so that you have taken at least a few seconds to experience each one. Another way is to go through them as you feel moved. If you are feeling the silence and then begin to feel that it is beautiful, then the beauty you feel can be your next focus. If you are focusing on the beauty and then feel a sense of kindness, then focus on the kindness next. I recommend that you take both approaches so that you are allowing yourself to be moved by whatever qualities arise, and also you are making sure you have focused on most of the qualities during your meditation session.

Gratitude for Anchors and Spiritual Qualities

Gratitude is such an important part of the spiritual life and can be a very effective practice during meditation. An article from gograteful.io speaks of the scientific evidence supporting the benefits of gratitude.

"Routinely practicing gratitude helps us experience increased positive emotions.

Gratitude increases dopamine and serotonin levels in the brain, which are key neurotransmitters that give us feelings of contentment. If we are grateful more often, the happiness-producing neural pathways strengthen, just as exercise strengthens the body.

Researchers from the University of California, Davis, and the University of Miami found that after regularly expressing gratitude for 10 weeks, study participants reported feeling more optimistic about their lives. Optimism, in turn, has been shown to be a life-lengthening trait in a recent Harvard University study."[18]

In this technique, we focus our gratitude on whatever is in our awareness as we meditate. The two main categories for this are meditation anchors (the moment, the breath, the body, the mind, etc.) and spiritual qualities such as peace, silence, happiness, kindness, etc. For this meditation, I would stay focused rather than be thankful for things such as friends, family, material things, past experiences, etc. There is definitely a benefit in being thankful for these things as well and I would encourage you to be grateful for them, but being focused just on anchors and spiritual qualities will help to keep you in the present moment, which is a very important aspect of meditation. If you begin expressing gratitude for a friend, for example, it is easier for the mind to wander and think about various things that you did with your friend.

There are a few ways to express or feel gratitude. If you believe in God you might express your gratitude directed that way. You might say, "Thank you for this peace, for this joy, this body, mind, breath, etc." Some people are more comfortable expressing gratitude to the universe or their "higher power," possibly in the same manner. Other people might prefer simply feeling gratitude without directing it toward any higher power. So it is entirely up to you depending on your beliefs and preferences. Whatever manner that you use, try to focus with your heart, and truly feel grateful. The benefits that you receive from this meditation are proportional to the feeling that you put into your expressions of gratitude.

As you sit and meditate you might begin by focusing on your breath, as you would do in breathing meditation, except adding the component of feeling gratitude for your breath, as well as feeling gratitude for the sensations that you feel as you breathe.

In like manner also take time to focus on your body as the object of meditation. As you do, feel gratitude for your body. Feel gratitude for how it feels and for whatever sensations arise as you focus on your body. You can even do a body scan and feel gratitude for each part of your body as you go through it.

You can feel gratitude for spiritual qualities as you feel them. Even if you don't feel certain spiritual qualities at the moment you can just be grateful that they are still within you. The following are more suggestions for objects of gratitude.

Anchors	Spiritual Qualities	
The breath	Peace	Calm
The body	Stillness	Beauty
The mind	Kindness	Gentleness
The present moment	Happiness	Joy
Awareness	Pureness	Power
	Silence	Love
	Sacredness	Bliss

CHAPTER 6
EXPANDING YOUR PRACTICE

Walking Meditation

 Another way to meditate is by walking at a very slow pace. This is normally done in a private place, such as your backyard or inside your home. A good focus during walking meditation is being mindful of your feet touching the ground. Just like breathing meditation, whenever your mind begins to wander, gently let go of the thoughts and bring your mind back to your breath. It is the same with focusing on the feet. When the mind wanders off you will bring it back to the sensation of the feet touching the ground. I find it helpful to think of my feet kindly or gently touching the ground with every step. It is also fine to notice your breath, your body, your mind, or the moment as you focus on your steps. You can be mindful of the wind blowing against your skin, the sun warming your body, and the grass on the ground. All this is fine if you are observing them mindfully and don't allow these things to become distractions.

Most of the meditations in Chapter 5 can also be done during walking meditation. A very effective practice is to apply Sacred Adjectives to each step. You might say something like this as you walk, "This is a beautiful step, this is a calm step, a gentle step, a sacred step, etc."

Walking meditation is a very effective tool, especially in conjunction with a long sitting meditation. I have been at some meditation sessions where they will meditate, while sitting, for 30 minutes, followed by a 10-minute walking meditation, and then another 30-minute sitting meditation. It has been my experience, with this format, that after the halftime walking meditation I feel quite re-energized for the final 30-minutes of sitting meditation. So this can be very effective at keeping you alert and also for keeping the body from getting too stiff from sitting too much.

Formal Retreats

One way to become more focused in your meditation practice is to spend more time in meditation with fewer distractions. Many groups that practice meditation will offer spiritual retreats from time to time. A retreat may last a day, a week, or even longer. Retreats often offer teachings as well. Walking meditations may be included too so that you don't become too stiff from sitting all day. In many retreats talking is not allowed. Some call this observing noble silence.

Scientists who study the effects of meditation have discovered that meditators who spend time at retreats obtain greater benefits. Here is a quote from the book "Altered Traits,"[19] by Daniel Goleman and Richard J. Davidson, discussing some of these benefits.

"… data suggests that meditating for one session daily is very different from a multiday or longer retreat. Take a finding that emerged unexpectedly in the study of seasoned meditators (9,000 average lifetime hours) and their reactivity to stress[20] … The stronger the connectivity between the meditators' prefrontal area and amygdala (a key node in the brain's stress circuitry), the less reactive they were. The surprise: the greatest increase in prefrontal-amygdala connection correlated with the number of hours a meditator had spent in retreat but not with home hours. Along these lines, another surprising finding was from the study of breath rate. A meditator's hours of retreat practice most strongly correlated with slower breathing, much more than daily practice."[21]

Personal Retreats

The importance of retreat time proved to be very significant to me after I experienced a few formal retreats. When I realized the impact it had on me I decided to do a personal one-day retreat once a week, by myself at home. I have set aside every Sunday for this purpose. It is the one day that I don't have any commitments so it is free of distractions. This gives me plenty of time to meditate and contemplate.

It is important to lay down some ground rules for a personal retreat day, such as no entertainment (TV, Netflix, most music, etc.). If you normally watch TV or Netflix while you sit down to eat, you can replace it with a teaching tape on a spiritual topic. YouTube is full of many insightful teachers. Instead of playing pop music while you are making yourself lunch, you can replace it with Native American flute music or the sounds of Tibetan singing bowls. These types of music are very soothing and they quiet the mind. Fortunately, in this day and age, we can find these types of music easily on the internet. There are many websites like Pandora that give free access to all kinds of music. Or you can prepare your meals and eat with complete silence and just be mindful of what you are doing. Practice being in the moment.

I try to do a fairly long meditation session on this day. I find that sitting for at least 90 minutes allows for insights to arise. When I know I might be sitting that long I will put a pad of paper and a pen next to me. This way if some insights do arise I can jot them down so that I don't forget what it was and then I continue to meditate. If you should try to meditate for this long you might want to use some of the "High Energy" meditation techniques that I described in   Chapter 5. Remember when you are alert use calming techniques and when you become drowsy use high-energy techniques.

Doing personal retreats doesn't have to be all meditation. There are certainly other effective practices you can incorporate. If you are like me you probably don't want to sit all day. I always make it a point to go for a walk during my retreat day. You can use the walk time to reflect on spiritual things. You can pray. You can be mindful as you walk. You can notice each step as a focus of meditation. In the following section, I share a contemplative practice that I like to use during my personal retreat day which I often practice during walks. It's a way of reflecting on quotes from inspirational authors or your own personal insights.

Another very valuable practice that I recommend for your personal retreat day is to spend about 30 minutes writing down things that you feel grateful for. When you write them down, put your heart into it. Try to feel a strong sense of gratitude. You can start by expressing gratitude for the basic necessities of life such as your income, your savings, food, car, home, heat, etc. You might think of things that you normally take for granted like sidewalks, streets, services like email, snail mail, books, clothes, etc. You can also go a bit deeper and express gratitude for family and friends; that great conversation you had with someone the other day, the hug a loved one gave you earlier, for the wonderful experiences you've had, for the accomplishments you made, and even for certain books you have read that have greatly influenced your life. You can give thanks for your capacity to feel love, kindness, peace, silence, happiness, joy, and bliss; for spiritual experiences, you may have had, such as stillness or bliss while in meditation. The list can go on and on and become more meaningful. Gratitude is indeed a very powerful practice.

The most obvious benefit that comes from a personal retreat day is that you simply dig deeper spiritually. Another benefit that I find is that it is like a vacation from the usual routine. After staying away from entertainment all day and being mostly silent, I find that the next day when I do go back to some of these things, I appreciate them more. When I see my friends I feel like I appreciate them more as well. I also feel refreshed and more excited about the new day. It's as if I've been out of town for a day and I'm excited to be back, and I'm ready to go!

Not everyone has the time to set aside an entire day for retreat. Another alternative is to set aside one to three hours once a week for a long meditation session. As I mentioned, with longer sessions you are more likely to get insights. It can also be beneficial in learning to overcome obstacles that happen during meditation, like sleepiness, for example. One evening while I was doing a four-day formal retreat we were having a one-hour evening meditation session. I was becoming very sleepy. From that need to keep from nodding off I came up with the "Infusion" technique that is in Chapter 5 under the "High Energy" section. That night I found it particularly effective to do the hand motions of that technique. After I did that for about ten to fifteen minutes I felt more awake and I was able to go back to more of a calming meditation without being sleepy.

If you are new to meditation, one to three hours might seem incomprehensible. You might even find it difficult to meditate for 10 minutes. The point is to stretch yourself a bit, but not to overwhelm yourself. If you are accustomed to meditating for 15 minutes at a time then once a week try to sit for 20 to 30 minutes. If you are used to sitting for 30 minutes, then try for 45 or 60 minutes and so on.

A Contemplation Practice

I would like to offer another practice that is a close cousin of meditation: contemplation. I have been doing a practice for many years, even before I became a meditator, which has been extremely beneficial to me. This practice makes use of index cards and some of your favorite spiritual quotes. Often, we may read a wonderful spiritual book that has plenty of wise advice, but after we read it we may remember just a few key points and end up forgetting quite a bit of the material that could be very useful. This practice can work as a follow-up to reading. It will help you to internalize the knowledge you have acquired and carry it forward into your daily life.

Start with 3 x 5 cards. Cut a number of them in half so you have cards that are 3 x 2.5. This is just the right size for one or two-sentence quotes that you will write on them. This size also fits nicely in your pocket. Start with one or two of your favorite spiritual books that you have read. Of course, it is extremely helpful if you underline or highlight as you read. If you do you can simply look for the sections that you have marked without having to read the whole book all over again. Then as you read through various underlined sections find some lines that really resonate with you. Then write them on the cards that you have prepared. If it doesn't fit on the card then it is too long. You want only one or two sentences that you can reflect on. Keep it short and simple.

A nice alternative to this preparation is to buy thick paper that is about the same thickness as the index cards. I use 180 lb paper that comes in standard 11 x 8.5" sheets. This can usually be found at most stores that specialize in office supplies. Then if you are good at using spreadsheets like Excel you can create your cards on the spreadsheet and print them on this paper. Then you would just have to cut the cards out for your use. I'm sure there are probably other apps you can use as well to do this.

Before my doctor told me to give up coffee I used to love to go to a coffee shop and sit at a table with these cards and pour through them. These days I like to bring them with me when I go for my daily walk. The point is, you can take them anywhere. If you are waiting in line at the grocery store you can pull them out of your pocket and use that time to reflect on them. I will usually just go through just one to three of them during a 30-minute walk. It's good to spend plenty of time just focusing on one or two sentences. It can be very insightful. Often when I am thinking about one of the quotes I will get insight and I will write down my thoughts. Frequently these insights will also be put on my cards. Now I have more cards that have my insights than I do of insights from authors that I have read. This is good because when it comes from within, it becomes more personal and more powerful, and therefore more transforming.

Mindfulness throughout the Day

Another important practice is to bring mindfulness into your everyday life. It's not easy to be mindful all the time, but there are certain activities that you do during your day that can be good for mindfulness practice. Washing the dishes, for instance. While you wash the dishes you can try to really focus on what you are doing. Be in the moment. Notice how it feels to wash them, how the soapy water feels. Think of it as a focus for meditation. Rather than letting your mind wander into all kinds of thought, just be in the moment experiencing the task. You can even use the act of eating as a mindfulness experience; mindfully tasting, mindfully chewing, etc.

It is also a good practice to pause off and on during the day just to notice the breath or notice what the body feels like. Pausing to be silent and mindful creates a sacred moment. You can stop for just a few seconds and ask yourself what this moment feels like, notice the sensations in your body, or observe the mind. You can pause to say the word "kindness" silently to yourself or to say some of the sacred adjectives from Chapter 5. You can remind yourself that this is a beautiful, precious moment. All these pauses help you to be more present, more relaxed, less chaotic, and more in control.

Mindfulness while Listening

One way to practice mindfulness that I consider to be extremely important is being mindful when you are listening to someone. Allow this person to be the primary focus of your attention just as when you meditate and use the breath as a focus. Try to be absorbed with everything that person is saying. Thich Nhat Hanh talks about "deep listening." This is being very focused on what the other person is saying. It includes listening with a heart of compassion.[22] Next time you are in a conversation; see what it is like to practice this. I'm not saying that all you do is listen and never say a word. It's certainly okay to talk, but when you are listening give the person your full attention. Thich Nhat Hanh suggests keeping this phrase in mind as you are listening to someone who is struggling. "I know you suffer, and that is why I am here for you."[23] In a short story by Leo Tolstoy called "The Three Questions" a wise hermit makes a profound statement, "The most important person is always the person with whom you are, who is right before you."[24] If we can have that attitude as we are paying attention we will truly be focused listeners.

We can listen to someone as if it were a meditation practice. What I mean is, when your friend has the floor, when she is talking, listen like you would if you were focusing on your breath in breathing meditation. When you do a meditation with the focus on your breath and your mind begins to wander, you simply bring your mind back to the breath over and over again. It is the same way when you listen. If you are listening and you begin to think about what you heard on the news earlier, bring your mind back to the focus of "the most important person," the person you are with right now. Many things can come up in your mind when you are listening. For example, you might wish you were somewhere else. If such a thought comes to mind, bring it back to this moment and the speaker. You might think of what you did earlier, or what you will do later. Again, bring the mind back to this moment and the speaker. You might even be judging your friend. You might think, "Why is he complaining, his situation is not so bad!" Again remind yourself to listen with compassion and let your mind be silent as you listen.

It is often tempting to mentally prepare what you are going to say in response to the speaker. Again, bring your mind back to your focus, the speaker. In his book, "The Seven Habits of Highly Effective People," Stephen R. Covey says, "Most people do not listen with the intent to understand; they listen with the intent to reply."[25] When we do this our mind is busy and we cannot listen deeply to the person before us. How will we respond effectively? It is better to simply trust that when our time comes to reply we will be more in tune with the speaker's situation because of our deep listening and it will be easier to reply as a result. If we still do not have an effective reply we can assure our friend that we are there for him. Often a person just needs someone to listen and by lending a compassionate ear they might figure out their problem for themselves.

You might be surprised to find out that this type of listening not only benefits the speaker but benefits the listener as well. In an article on mindtools.com entitled, "Mindful Listening, Developing Awareness to Listen Fully," some benefits of mindful listening are examined. The following quote is referring to Rebecca Z. Shafir, author of the book, "The Zen of Listening," and Charlie Scott author of the book "Get Out of Your Own Head: Mindful Listening for Project Managers."

"Shafir and Scott... suggest mindful listening can potentially have physical and psychological benefits. Shafir likens focusing on another person to stroking a pet – you forget about yourself, your blood pressure drops, and you feel calmer. And Scott says it can reduce anxiety and increase positive feelings."[26]

To share from my personal experience, on a few occasions, some time ago, when I was struggling with a problem, I would call a close friend and we would go out to get a cup of coffee and talk. I would have in mind that this is a great opportunity for me to talk about my problem. However when we sat down to talk my friend would say, "You know I'm glad we are getting together tonight because I'm really struggling with something. Would you mind if I got some things off my chest?" Well, how could I say "no?" So I end up listening to my friend's problems and before I know it, I forget what I was so worked up about. Once I got my mind off myself for a while I realized that my problem was not so big. I was just blowing things out of proportion. This has happened a few times that I can remember. This is not to say that you should never talk things out when you do have problems. No, it is good to talk things out at times when the time is right.

SUMMARY

When I began my inner journey of meditation several years ago, I had trouble meditating for just a few minutes without feeling like I was about to nod off. I did, however, experience some glimpses of peace and silence that felt right. Then after some years of practice, I started feeling some very beautiful feelings during meditation of love and kindness. I can remember many times when I would exclaim "There is so much love!" This was in response to the love I felt within, which seemed to spontaneously emerge from the silence. I began to realize that meditation wakes you up to what is within you.

Many of the meditations that I shared in Chapter 5 use lists with adjectives or nouns that are lofty, wholesome, and beautiful. An interesting phenomenon has occurred in my life from the practice of using some of these words as a focus in my meditation sessions. I will be going about my business and suddenly, as if from nowhere, I find myself saying the word "kindness," and truly feeling the kindness within. It puts a whole new spin on the phrase "heart attack." I like to call these occurrences "kindness attacks." It's a beautiful pause that wells up within me the more I meditate. I will walk to the kitchen to do the dishes and I feel a warm sense of kindness within me. I may grab my chest, but don't call an ambulance. It's not heart failure. No, it's something beautiful; it's a "kindness attack." This type of kind experience that happens off the meditation cushion is a testimony as to how, through the training of meditation, the brain becomes rewired.

The word "beautiful," which is frequently used in some of my meditations, often comes up spontaneously even when I am not meditating, as if from nowhere. I will spontaneously note that "This moment is beautiful." The mind is being rewired by the practice of meditation to think more positive, wholesome thoughts.

This is so important when we consider how often our thoughts are normally very negative by default. Much of this negativity is picked up as children and becomes our programming through the rest of our life. Meditation is a powerful tool to help reprogram these negative thought patterns even after a lifetime of negative programming.

I hope that you have benefited from this book in some way. I hope it causes you to become more excited about meditation and make it a regular practice; or that you have learned some new techniques that help you to go deeper. Or perhaps you might be inspired to create some of your own techniques.

May your meditations be sublime and bring insight and peace into your life.

John Moeller
Colorado Springs, CO
2022

If this book was meaningful to you, please review it on Amazon.com. Your review might encourage others to read it and benefit from it. Thank you.

WORKS CITED

CHAPTER 1

[1]Dienstmann, Giovanni."Types of Meditation — An Overview of 23 Meditation Techniques." *Live & Dare*, https://liveanddare.com/types-of-meditation/, para. 3, (accessed 17 June 2022)

CHAPTER 2

[2]Om Swami, *A Million Thoughts*. India, Jaico Publishing House, Worldwide publishing rights: Black Lotus Press, 2016, [Kindle Version], Retrieved from Amazon.com, Chapter title: Mental Exertion and Relaxation, para. 11.

[3]Om Swami, *A Million Thoughts* [Kindle Version]. Retrieved from Amazon.com, Chapter title: When Thoughts Become Things, last para.

[4]Hahn, Thich Nhat. *You Are Here: Discovering the Magic of the Present Moment*. Escondido, CA, Shambhala Publications, Inc, 2009, [Kindle Version], Retrieved from Amazon.com, Ch. 4, para. 13.

5 Hahn, Thich Nhat. "Turn Every Cell On." Online video clip. *YouTube: Plum Village*, 2005, Plum Village, https://www.youtube.com/watch?v=jrncYE3g4oc, 21:04-25:50 (accessed 17 June 2022).

6Brahm, Ajahn. "Anapanasati." Online video clip. *YouTube: B*, 2020, https://www.youtube.com/watch?v=5jOd1Sbo_ow, 12:16-17:03, (accessed 17 June 2022).

7Mascaro, Juan, translator. *The Bhagavad Gita*. The Penguin Group, 1962, [Kindle Version], Retrieved from Amazon.com, Chapter 2, Verse 65.

8Goleman, Daniel and Richard Davidson, "How Meditation Changes Your Brain - and Your Life." *Lion's Roar,* 2018, Avery, an imprint of Penguin Publishing Group, a division of Penguin Random House LLC, https://www.lionsroar.com/how-meditation-changes-your-brain-and-your-life/?fbclid=IwAR0WXvqN6E65k5CPNLvnP41xB5f_29Xog qqoI5VJsfwzJmH5Fft5T4BTSLQ, (accessed 14 June 2022), para. 1, (accessed 17 June 2022).

9Goleman, Daniel and Richard Davidson. Altered Traits: Science Reveals Meditation Changes Your Mind. Brain, and Body. Penguin Random House LLC, New York NY, 2017.

[10]Mascaro, Juan, translator. *The Bhagavad Gita*. The Penguin Group, 1962, [Kindle Version], Retrieved from Amazon.com, Chapter 6, Verse 10.

CHAPTER 4

[11]Brahm, Ajahn. "'Peace-o-meter' Guided Meditation." Online video clip. *YouTube: Budding Buddha, 2019*, https://www.youtube.com/watch?v=DpYa2X-tHEY, 8:12-56, (accessed 14 July 2022).

CHAPTER 5

[12]Mascaro, Juan, translator. *The Bhagavad Gita*. [Kindle Version], Retrieved from Amazon.com, Chapter 17, Verse 16.

[13]Mascaro, Juan, Translator. *The Bhagavad Gita*. [Kindle Version], Retrieved from Amazon.com, Chapter 5, Verses 27-28.

[14] Mascaro, Juan, Translator. *The Bhagavad Gita*. [Kindle Version], Retrieved from Amazon.com, Chapter 9, Verses 22.

[15]Rurayamala, Translated from Sanskrit by Mike Magee, "Vijnanabhairava Tantra." *Shiva Shakti Mandalam,* 1975-2022, https://shivashakti.com/vijnan, verse 42, (accessed 14 June 2022).

[16]Campbell, Joseph, and Bill Moyers, The Power of Myth. New York NY, Anchor Books, A division of Random House, Inc, 1991.

[17]Om Swami, A Million Thoughts [Kindle Version]. Retrieved from Amazon.com, Chapter title: Mental Exertion and Relaxation, para. 2.

[18]Dineshkumar, Presh. "The Power of Gratitude." *GoGrateful,* https://www.gograteful.io/gratitude/the-power-of-gratitude, para. 4, 2019

CHAPTER 6

[19]Goleman, Daniel, and Richard Davidson, *Altered Traits: Science Reveals Meditation Changes Your Mind. Brain, and Body.* Penguin Random House LLC, New York, NY,

2017, [Kindle Version], Retrieved from Amazon.com, Chapter 13, Section: Expertise, para. 7.

This paragraph, quoted from Altered Traits, has its own citations. These are referred to as "notes" They are located near the end of the book. The following indented notes are " word for word" from Altered Traits, Notes: Chapter 14, Notes 7 and 8

[20]E. G. Patsenko et al., "Resting State (rs)-fMRI and Diffusion Tensor Imaging (DTI) Reveals Training Effects of a Meditation-Based Video Game on Left Fronto-Parietal Attentional Network in Adolescents," submitted 2017.

[21]B. L. Alderman et al., "Mental and Physical (MAP) Training: Combining Meditation and Aerobic Exercise Reduces Depression and Rumination while Enhancing Synchronized Brain Activity," Translational Psychiatry 2 (accepted for publication 2016) e726–9; doi:10.1038/tp.2015.225.

[22]Hahn, Thich Nhat. The Art of Communicating. Harper One, An Imprint of Harper Collins Publishers, 2013, [Kindle Version], Retrieved from Amazon.com, Chapter 3, Section: The Keys to Compassionate Communication.

[23]Hahn, Thich Nhat. The Art of Communicating. Harper One, An Imprint of Harper Collins Publishers, 2013, [Kindle Version], Retrieved from Amazon.com, Chapter 4, Section: The Third Mantra, para 1.

[24]Tolstoy, Leo. 'The Three Questions.' *Plough*, https://www.plough.com/en/topics/culture/short-stories/the-three-questions, last para., (accessed 14 July 2022).

[25]Covey, Steven R. The 7 Habits of Highly Effective People. New York NY, Simon & Schuster, 1989, p. 239.

[26]Mind Tools Content Team, "Mindful Listening: Developing Awareness to Listen Fully." *Mind Tools*, https://www.mindtools.com/pages/article/mindful-listening.htm, Section: What are the Benefits of Mindful Listening? last para., (accessed 14 July 2022).

ABOUT THE AUTHOR

 John Moeller has practiced daily meditation for over nine years, and he continually tries techniques from various religions and disciplines, and constantly develops new ones. He attends The Web of Connection, which is a Theravada Buddhist community in Colorado Springs, where he serves on the board, writes their weekly emails, and leads a weekly guided meditation. John has explored various spiritual teachings and does not consider himself to be a member of any particular religion; he finds benefits from the teachings of most religions.

He has a bachelor's degree in Geography from the New Mexico State University, and an associate's degree in Geographic Information Technology from Central New Mexico Community College. He has been self-employed for the past twelve years as a stock trader.

You can read his weekly emails, which are posted on the Web of Connection's website:

https://www.webofconnection.com/weekly-bulletin.html

They provide the current schedule for his weekly guided meditation including the Zoom link. They also provide information about Web of Connection events and frequently include spiritual insights.

Made in the USA
Las Vegas, NV
10 May 2024

89784659R00046